All the Wasted Beauty of the World

ALL THE WASTED BEAUTY OF THE WORLD

POEMS BY
RICHARD
NEWMAN

ABLE MUSE PRESS

Able Muse Press

www.ablemusepress.com

Printed in the United States of America

Library of Congress Control Number: 2014938397

ISBN 978-1-927409-31-2 (paperback)
ISBN 978-1-927409-32-9 (digital)

Cover image: "Great Blue Heron of Southern Indiana" by Nick Nihira

Cover & book design by Alexander Pepple

Able Muse Press is an imprint of *Able Muse:* A Review of Poetry, Prose & Art—at www.ablemuse.com

Able Muse Press
467 Saratoga Avenue #602
San Jose, CA 95129

for Shanie Latham

Acknowledgments

I am grateful to the editors of the following journals where many of these poems originally appeared, sometimes in earlier versions.

Anti-: "Alley Possum," "4 a.m.," "White Pebble, Shell, and Feather: Spell for Finding Lost Things."

Birmingham Poetry Review: "The Ugliest Woman Sitting at the Bar."

Boulevard: "Bricks," "Digging Up the Elephant Ears," "Hiker's Trail Guide for Lost Man Pass (7 mi.)," "Ode to Big Muddy Asian Carp," "Stopping for Lunch Near Goshen, Indiana," "Surprise."

Briar Cliff Review: "Once More to the Roof Deck."

Crab Orchard Review: "Wild Turkey in January," "Ode to the Urban Mulberry."

Garbanzo!: "Gossip," "Wee Hours."

I-70 Review: "April Morning."

Iron Horse Literary Review: "Rat King."

JMWW: "Aubade," "Perfect Pearl: Spell for Luck."

The Ledge: "Bellefontaine Cemetery."

The Louisville Review: "Man Accidentally Locks Himself in Basement," "Necromancy Spell."

Measure: "New Harmony, Indiana, with a Refrain Once Spoken There by John Hawkes," "Overture from *The Lost City.*"

Midwestern Gothic: "Lullaby for the Benton Park Homeless Population."

Natural Bridge: "Bloom of Light: Winter Spell to Revitalize Your Spirit When Days Are Dark and Gloom Settles Upon You."

Poems & Plays: "Italian Sonnet," "Ode to Despair."

Poetry East: "Four Kids Pissing off the Overpass after a Cardinals Game," "Great Blue Heron of Southern Indiana."

Sou'wester: "Oblivion," "Picnic Pavilion in a State Park."

UCity Review: "Double Helix," "Ode to the Brown-Banded Cockroach."

Unsplendid: "Three Triolets on Lines from Public Places."

Valparaiso Review: "Old Lady at the Beach."

"Bellefontaine Cemetery" won First Place in *The Ledge* 2010 Poetry Awards. "4 a.m.," "Gossip," and "Wee Hours" also appeared in the chapbook *24 Tall Boys: Dark Verse for Light Times* (Snark Publishing/Firecracker Press, 2007). "Wild Turkey in January" also appeared in the anthology *Small Batch* (Two of Cups Press, 2013). "Please Be Advised" appeared in *Flood Stage: An Anthology of St. Louis Poets* (Walrus Publishing, 2010).

I am grateful to the Regional Arts Commission for the Individual Artist Fellowship that made completing this book possible.

Thanks to all the friends and family who have helped with this book: Chas Adams, James Arthur, Scott Berman, Richard Burgin, The CharFlies, Amy Clark, Brian Cochran, Andy Cox, the good people at Doctor's Cave, Danny Elfanbaum, Jen Fandel, Jim and Maia Funkhouser, Ginger, Joanne Lowery, Kimberly Lozano, Adrian Matejka, Meghan McEnery, Kara Moyer, Kerry and Ricki Newman, Nick Nihira, Alex Pepple, Qiu Xiaolong, Jessica Rogen, Steve Schreiner (who should have been thanked in the last book), Steven D. Schroeder, Tina Yellow Ranger Shen, Catherine Tufariello, and Uncle Larry. Most special love and appreciation for Shanie Latham, Natalie Newman, and Tanya Seale.

The lotus blossom losing its aroma
and its leaves fading in verdancy,
the west wind sighing and vexing
the green ripples,
it is unbearable to see
the beauty ravaged by time.

In a drizzle, a dream returns
to the far-away frontier.
A melody keeps arising out of the tiny tower
until the jade flute turns too cold
for the player to continue.

—Li Jing (916-961), translated by Qiu Xiaolong

Contents

Acknowledgments   *vi*

1. SUMMER SPELLS

Ode to the Urban Mulberry   *3*
Hiker's Trail Guide for Lost Man Pass (7 mi.)   *5*
Old Lady at the Beach   *7*
Lullaby for the Benton Park
      Homeless Population   *8*
Four Kids Pissing off the Overpass
      after a Cardinals Game   *10*
New Harmony, Indiana, with a Refrain
      Once Spoken There by John Hawkes *11*
Alley Possum   *13*
Perfect Pearl: Spell for Luck   *14*
Three Triolets on Lines from Public Places   *16*
Italian Sonnet   *18*
Once More to the Roof Deck   *19*

2. AUTUMN CONTRAILS

Great Blue Heron of Southern Indiana   *23*
Digging Up the Elephant Ears   *24*
At the St. Louis Symphony Season Premiere   *26*
Overture from *The Duchesses of Devonshire*   *27*
Rat King   *30*
4 a.m.   *31*
Aubade   *33*

White Pebble, Shell, and Feather:
    Spell for Finding Lost Things   *35*
Oblivion   *37*
Wee Hours   *38*
Bricks   *40*

3. Winter's Bloom

Wild Turkey in January   *45*
Ode to Despair   *47*
Bloom of Light: Winter Spell to Revitalize
    Your Spirit When Days Are Dark
        and Gloom Settles Upon You   *49*
Double Helix   *51*
The Ugliest Woman Sitting at the Bar   *52*
Ode to the Brown-Banded Cockroach   *53*
Please Be Advised   *55*
Stopping for Lunch Near Goshen, Indiana   *56*

4. Spring Necromancies

Ode to Big Muddy Asian Carp   *61*
Picnic Pavilion in a State Park   *63*
Man Accidentally Locks Himself in Basement   *64*
Surprise   *66*
Gossip   *67*
Overture from *The Lost City*   *69*
Necromancy Spell   *72*
April Morning   *74*
Bellefontaine Cemetery   *75*

All the Wasted Beauty of the World

1. Summer Spells

Ode to the Urban Mulberry

Our mothers told us you were poisonous
so we might not come home stained with summer.
Junk tree. Weed grown thick as an old man's wrist.
We yank you from our gutters, gardens, lawns,
and sidewalk cracks you widen into grins
and toothless yawns.

Mutt plant—genitals dangling purple, black,
red, pink, and white. You sticky the very ground
from which you sprang. Slut fruit. Jackberry,
prized only by the innocent,
your leaves like mittens in the lost and found.
You seed, you burst—even between our bricks
you feed on air and mortar and won't relent.

A galaxy of gnats twists in your shade.
Birds love to scattershit you on our cars.
We hose you off as Kool-Aid rinse. Craptree.
One neighbor exorcised a hard life's worth
of hate on you with saw and axe.
Your white strain crossed both oceans, took up root
to feed your leaves to fussy Chinese silkworms,
then spread through shit of rats, raccoons, and possums
and bumbled up with native reds and blacks.

While walking home, we check that no one's watching,
reach over a neighbor's fence or through the bars,
and pluck your ripest, darkest fruit—sweet,
insipid—so little taste for all your stains
on fingers, tongues, then gone, a moment
of summer, sweet poisons pushing through our veins.

Hiker's Trail Guide for Lost Man Pass (7 mi.)

The trail before you, tacking and turning through
the mountain pass, was once a road, now sheared
and crumbling down the boulder slope to the creek.
You'll likely see no animals but notice
piles of fresh droppings, left as if for spite.
You might grow breathless in thin mountain air
but want to see what lies beyond each bend,
what waits for you at the top where it begins
to flatten, and as you climb the old road wound,
narrowed into a scar of trail, you'll weave
through crowding evergreens and black-eyed Susans.
There you may see, if sharp-eyed, in a gully,
a Ford truck from the 1920s, home
to a hundred generations of bugs and birds,
the engine choked with vines, its passengers
stretching their green limbs and leaves through windows,
the whole truck rusting fleck by golden fleck
into the ravine. You might stand a moment
searching for the humor or irony,
then notice that the forest sounds have stopped—
all birdsong, trill of insects, swallowed by
silence except the sounds of your own breathing,
and you may wonder if you're predator
or prey, if our destruction of this savage,
innocent world is also part of nature.
The woods will soon forget that you are there,
as locusts ratchet up the afternoon

intensity and gnats swarm for your sweat,
and you sit down on a fallen tree to watch
the mountain gnaw on a pile of old Ford bones.

Old Lady at the Beach

Her pilgrimage is like those old Saharan
films where the doomed figure staggers up dune
after dune, knowing like us the end is soon
but nonetheless keeps stumbling through this barren
world—to what exactly? Salvation? Water?
And now she passes all the couples, hand
in hand or trading rubdowns, supremely tanned.
She focuses on her three-legged totter,
ignoring children, too, who burrow grain
by grain to China. So many holes and hassles!
She continues her assault upon the sands,
stepping on blankets, squashing fresh sandcastles.
Deaf to the children's gull-like cries, she stands
knee-deep and slashes at the waves with her cane.

Lullaby for the Benton Park
Homeless Population

For you who doze on church steps
or make camp in the park,
who've staked a bed of composted leaves
before the day grew dark,

who squat beneath the footbridge
and savor warm beer and gin,
who take in this whole neighborhood
though no one takes you in,

who wash off in the duck ponds
and sleep among swan turds,
I've nothing at all to offer you
but drifts of useless words.

The fish fry in our skillets.
The air grows thick with grease.
The moon melts in the hot black sky
and drips on drowsy police.

You have no need for my sorry,
but I offer it all the same.
From my porch I recognize your faces
but know not a single name.

May you score a fifth of bourbon
and find your stomach full,
and share a night's companionship
that's not inside your skull.

Find rest behind our dumpster,
safe passage in our alley,
where glaciers scraped this path you take
in the Mississippi Valley,

where barges bellow from mudbanks,
a train moans on its track,
and though your day's too wide to cross,
night always takes you back.

Four Kids Pissing off the Overpass
after a Cardinals Game

The highway floods with headlights from the game
while four streams arc over the concrete rail
and glimmer in the night as they take aim.
Victory is not calling Mom from jail,
provoking a Lexus' windshield wiper,
scoring another flask of Jameson
and Salems. Our lives span diaper to diaper,
and in between we piss on anyone
we can, in this case anyone with tickets.
Cops! Unzipped and dribbling on their shoes
they sprint away and climb a chain link fence,
then laugh, pass whiskey in the alley thickets—
princes of endless now, nothing to lose
but stupid summer jobs and innocence.

New Harmony, Indiana, with a Refrain
Once Spoken There by John Hawkes

*Location of two attempts at communal living: The
Harmonists under Reverend George Rapp, 1814-1825,
and the Owenites under philanthropist Robert Owen,
1825-1826.*

—Historic Marker

A costumed woman from the trailer park
dips greasy candles. When burned they never last.
The shadows of history are long and dark.

A bearded blacksmith hammers a sluggish spark
and flickers between the future and the past.
The people from the nearby trailer park

hear dogs across the Wabash howl and bark.
In cemeteries, thinning tombstones cast
shadows of history, long and dark.

Black hats, wool coats, or halters—the dress is stark.
Prospects for the future have long passed.
The old men from the nearby trailer park

meet at The Hornet, drink Bud and Maker's Mark.
They work hard and drink hard. Nothing's half-assed.
The shadows of history are long and dark.

Each decade, guests at the Marriott remark
on simpler times, good old days fading fast,
to locals from the nearby trailer park.
The shadows of history are long and dark.

Alley Possum

Fellow urbanite, how could your race
survive—convinced I can't see you this close,
hunched next to our back porch, your grinning face
hidden behind a bag of Ranch Doritos.
In our next-door neighbors' headlights, your eyes shine
Heineken green, and you keep eating, heedless.
You forage in the cracks of our lives and dine
on our debris, jaws crammed with infected needles.
By day you play dead in a dumpster—poke
you with a stick, your whole being explodes.
Primordially stupid, tireless joke,
you waddle down the shoulders of our roads,
loot gardens, lie in our bed of impatiens,
finding the hidden gaps in our foundations.

Perfect Pearl: Spell for Luck

materials: 1 whole, perfect pearl

1 piece of cobweb, freshly collected

1 acorn

1 saltshaker

*Under a new moon before dawn, place the first three
items before you, moon at your right shoulder. Sprinkle
salt generously around yourself in a three-foot diameter.
Concentrate on where in your life you most want luck to
land while invoking this incantation:*

Oh luck of sunshining summer shower,
impart to me your luck this hour,
of salted earth on sacred ground,
this lucky pearl in the palm of my hand,
this perfect world that spins around
a lucky grain of sand.

Bring me the luck from buttons of bone,
the luck of a hand-warmed pocket stone.
Lend me the luck the cricket sings,
the inside-out white dress or blouse,
the luck a blushing robin brings
when it swoops into the house,

the luck of numbers, crooked and prime,
the once-kicked penny, the fountain dime,
the luck that creaks from a wooden stair,
the spit-shined luck and luck that glints
off a long and golden strand of hair
waving from a wooden fence,

the luck locked in the nut and seed,
braided in the mane of a midnight steed.
So luck will flow and luck will ebb,
but I catch your luck before day's begun
into this dew-strung spider web
from which this spell is spun.

Three Triolets on Lines from Public Places

1. Over the Airport Intercom

Robert MacGregor, please return to your wife
who's waiting with your baggage at the gate.
You cannot fly for long out of your life,
Robert MacGregor. Please return to your wife.
A little big with boredom and stained from strife,
she wears a pressed resilience to compensate.
Robert MacGregor—please. Return to your wife.
She's waiting with your baggage at the gate.

2. At a Cardinals Game in Busch Stadium

Will you please marry me, Katrina?
We're blinking on the JumboTron!
Since my love's big as this arena,
will you please marry me, Katrina?
Drunk Cubs fans snicker like hyenas.
You won't wait till the Cards have won,
will you? Please marry me, Katrina.
We're blinking on the JumboTron.

3. Missed Connections on Craigslist

You drove a white Impala heading west.
I waved and you waved back. You looked so pretty.
In that white flash my life was cursed and blessed.
You drove a white Impala. Heading west,
each white Impala stabs me in the chest.
I've posted ads like this throughout the city:
you drove a white Impala heading west.
I waved and you waved back. You looked so pretty.

Italian Sonnet

for J. P.

He taught a course in Florence for the summer,
didn't come back, and told her, "It's not you—
it's all this honeyed light." "One thing is true,"
she mused. "You've never said anything dumber."
She took the house. He never heard from her
again. His second wife and he soon flew
back home to Pine Lawn, a cabin and a view.
Next year she drove off in their brand new Hummer
to start an Italian bakery in L.A.
Her aim was alimony, which his first wife
never considered. His second made him pay
the remainder of his long, overcast life.
He never flinched, never put up a fight.
At least he'd held, if briefly, that honeyed light.

Once More to the Roof Deck

The boarded-up brick house across the alley,
where feral cats and teenagers make nests,
bows and yields to the slow pull of nature,
tosses out bricks, surrenders roof to trees.

The backyard has no grass blades but a carpet
of violets, strawberries, and dandelions.
A porch off Amber's home next door looks on,
so she and her new boy peel back the plywood

warped at the cellar door and crawl inside,
ignoring nails and generations of dust.
Geese argue in the pond across the street
as we watch from our roof deck, drink Bordeaux

that nibbles at the outskirts of our brains.
An alley tabby cries, "Hello? Hello?"
We call her Hello Kitty. Inside the house
another mewls and Amber moans on a mattress.

The moon and stars dissolve in city lights,
long summer night, scantily-clouded sky.
It's midnight—*ching!*—we toast to nothing new
beneath the sun but also nothing old

beneath our waning moon. We scratch and breathe.
The crickets scratch and breathe, and alley cats
rub up against the soothing bark of trees
as all of us disperse in the warm night air.

2. Autumn Contrails

Great Blue Heron of Southern Indiana

This gangly king, somber comedian
stretches his S-trap neck and Tinkertoy legs
and scours the grassy highway median,
spearing crawdaddies, frogs, hamburger pickles.
He stalks the muddy banks, peers through the dregs
of ditches which seep into the Blue, which trickles
into the brown Ohio. Cumulus
clouds straggle across the Indiana skies
asterisked with contrails. He doesn't flinch
at tractors or the orange-jumpsuited crowd
milling across the freeway or those proud,
suspicious hawks that pinwheel into semis
while his long toes meticulously inch
between the graceful and ridiculous.

Digging Up the Elephant Ears

"If you can't love each other, just pretend,"
my mother begged my younger brother and me,
who punched each other in back of our Impala.

I couldn't help but think of them today
when digging up the elephant ears—bright stalks
arcing six feet into the air each summer
and leaves the size of banquet platters that nod
languidly in breezes and condescend
to human heights only in August heat,

and yet they rise from ugly hearts, their gnarled
pink-tentacled bulbs that split to colonize
more earth and multiply in dirty broods.
They are the opposite of us, who must
force ourselves to dig beneath each other's
ugliness for hearts that hint of goodness
and love, and after first frost rarely bother.

But we must love each other, our betters say,
even the student who showed up to class
in a tight T-shirt that read *Fuck 'em all—
let my ovaries sort it out*. Especially her,
and the one who told the dean I showed up drunk,
which I have yet to do. My brother quit
drinking, I'm told—I haven't spoken to
my mother or my brother in seven years
since we no longer bother to pretend.

Each fall I am a brute and hack fine limbs,
pitching the hearts in garbage bins for winter.
Both front and back yards now are full of holes,
the stalks and ears wilting on compost piles.

My neighbor stumbles drunk down the alley.
Beneath his dirt and puke I sometimes see
the good. Sometimes it's easier to pretend.
Squirrels salvage the last of this year's garden
while silence gathers in the eastern skies,
the last few ears bending to strains of air.

At the St. Louis Symphony Season Premiere

The old men at the symphony take a *largo*
to piss. Bells chime the end of intermission.
"One of us should endow another john,"
says a tuxedoed, pecker-hunched patrician.
Another shoots back, "I don't think Wells Fargo
will match-grant johns." They laugh and piddle on.

A few stand on the sidewalk to smoke cigars,
sip pinot noir or scotch, cough a last cough,
then toss their glowing butts into the gutter.
A bus stops at the light—no one gets off.
Night shifters stare down blankly. Idling cars
thump hip-hop loud enough to make hearts flutter.

These once hard-working men of vigorous leisure
now nod to sleep. Their offspring play Nintendo
deep in red velvet chairs. Another head
succumbs to *grave* before the slow crescendo,
which maestros plotted from the first measure
to wake if not the living at least the dead.

Overture from *The Duchesses of Devonshire*

*for Georgiana Cavendish, Duchess of Devonshire,
1757-1806, first wife of William Cavendish, 5th Duke
of Devonshire*

Love, loss—
such puny words
to hold the worlds of joy and pain in me—
such paltry words
as love and loss, conception to decay—
I've known more forms of love than there are species
of scavengers
and birds of prey.

I love my hats,
each dainty shoe,
but I would lose
them all for you.
(And you and you and you!)

I introduced my best friend to my husband,
the old, cold, distant Duke of Devonshire,
and now she's moved into our home. By day
we walk the gardens arm in arm. At night
I hear them split the darkness down the hall.
Bess stomachs him as I do alcohol.

Votes for kisses
and love for hire,
when drunk I set
my wigs on fire.
(A dazzling attire!)

We love like willow witches divine water.
Dead sticks in hand, we wander and believe
we'll feel the elemental tug and totter.

Like those who name the gentle beasts they'll slaughter,
we love those most whom we must come to grieve,
and love like willow witches dowsing water,

give up our own yet raise another's daughter.
Love starts and ends in loss—don't be naïve
or shun the elemental tug and totter.

The heart remembers.
The womb forgets.
My love runs deeper
than my gambling debts.
(Grave losses, no regrets.)

I'd meet my love,
Charles Grey, in Bath,
where we'd make love
and love's aftermath:
a child, a husband's wrath.

I've raised all the duke's children as my own,
both our three chicks and Charlotte from the maid,
and not one of them would I trade for a life
with my Earl Grey, with whom I had Eliza.
I visit secretly, forced to give her away.
She now lives as a sister of Charles Grey.

I stand alone as my own alma mater,
deliver half the kisses I conceive,
and love like willow witches search for water.

I held my sparrow close. In faith, I taught her
forked branches often twitch for naught, deceive,
caught in the elemental tug and totter.

And all is not in vain,
not in vain if you turn your eyes from yourself
and love the world and all its birds of prey,
and love the world, its blue skies drained to gray,
for all is not in vain. You have not lived
until you've loved and lost and loved again
and again.

Rat King

A knot of fear and tendons, we have blundered,
tangled our tails in blood and dirt and shit
until we've grown together now as one
omnivorous frenzy with no will to stop,
swirling slowly to oblivion.
We tug and tear, know what it means to commit.
You, outsiders, we sicken and horrify.
A horde of mischief scuttling on a hundred
miniscule feet, our mob-ring twirls and hovers
down sewers, lost foundations built by Romans,
sometimes through wheat fields like a seething mop
that leaves a trail of disease, evil omens.
A fine excruciating way to die,
twisted with your family and lovers!

4 a.m.

This is the hour of food poisoning,
of car alarms
and firearms,
of someone creaking up the stairs.
4 a.m., the digital glares,
the hour when
wrong numbers ring,
sore throats begin,
drunk exes make their drunken calls,
a dog starts barking down the street.
The lumpy pillow, sweaty sheet,
and through the thin apartment walls
a neighbor loudly hacking phlegm
will always come at 4 a.m.
So many hours we've spent fretting
the praise that so-and-so is getting,
the good not given, love not taken
at 4 a.m. when we awaken,
the work not done, the bills not paid
(and yet not doing it or paying them).
The endless piss,
a night of drinking's dehydration,
and diarrhea, constipation—
all rouse themselves at 4 a.m.
Would James Bond lie awake like this?
A godless hour,
the stomach sour,

again the digital red glare,
and we are suddenly aware
of birdsong filling up the skies
and blue beginning at last to creep
through curtains, blinds, and half-closed eyes
and with some luck fall back asleep.

Aubade

We work all day and drink all night
beneath the stars on our back porch.
At four we watch the cold blue light
outline the brewery and Baptist church—
the same slow dawn if we were dead
and not about to fall in bed
begins the same, reddening climb
across the city's dingy skies,
and I realize
I'm good to go at any time.

It is perhaps a selfish thought.
What of my daughter and my wife?
Me: a burrito in slow rot,
the world's rearrangement of life.
To them I offer gratitude
for riding love's vicissitudes,
and friends who've seen me at the brink
shared better ways of being alone—
or being alone
together for a laugh and drink.

I squint at the nothingness that lies
beyond, not crap about a next
life or the childish fantasies
in TV ads or sacred texts
about a glorious hereafter.

I hope I'll leave behind more laughter
than sadness—not having followed fashion
or cash, or worked the kind of work
that enriched some jerk,
but showed a skeptical compassion.

Children and old folks fear the unknown,
and even more the rest of us
suspect down in our hollowing bones
what the unknown shrouds: nothingness.
Death's nothing is no horror—it's
the nothing in life that is the pits.
Life should be chugged like fine champagne—
I'll live my life until it hurts
and for my desserts
choose untold nothing over pain.

Meanwhile the bars have long since closed.
Out front a woman clicks to her car
in short black skirt and dulled stilettos,
her blonde hair steeped in cheap cigar.
This night, she knows deep in her heart, meant
nothing. She drives to her apartment.
The headlights on her Volvo sweep
our home. We stumble down the hall,
take hands and fall
into long, uninterrupted sleep.

White Pebble, Shell, and Feather:
Spell for Finding Lost Things

materials: 1 small white pebble, smoothed
by time and elements
1 white shell washed onto a beach
or riverbank
1 white feather
patch of earth among perennials
(flowers or herbs)
red wine

*Carry the three white objects in your pocket for three days. At
midnight, under a waxing moon, bury them in the earth. Pour one
chalice of wine over the earth, then one for yourself. Concentrate on
your missing object while invoking this incantation three times:*

Old keeper of what disappears,
return to me what once was mine
before it burrows under years,
relinquishes all shape and shine.

Before it knows the gnaw of rust,
the fangs of heat, the claw of frost,
succumbs to cobwebs, falls to dust,
return to me what I have lost.

Return what was more dear to me
than stolen kisses from loves past,
than sunlight scraped across the sea,
for nothing in this world will last.

I offer three things found, my debt,
and bind this spell with draughts of wine.
If you will not let me forget,
return to me what once was mine.

Oblivion

Before his wife has even boarded the plane,
he's booked a Days Inn room and called an ex
to drown his solitude with drink and sex.
On nights when she's in town they sit and drain
drink after drink in poolside chairs, their lives
a blurring haze of smoke and vodka tonic.
Upstairs their teenaged daughter, dark, ironic,
crosshatches her thin arms with kitchen knives—
forearms she hides with bracelets and long sleeves,
dull pain that only sharper pain relieves.
Her brother surfs for porn holes, fingers curled
around himself, ogling the end of the world,
and each night blessed oblivion will shine
through sweating tumblers, flesh, and blood design.

Wee Hours

Drunkenness shouts and staggers,
and thinks it is a riot
pinballing down our alley.
Shame creeps nice and quiet.

Drunkenness breaks beer bottles,
slugs shoulders, and kicks cans.
Shame keeps keys from jangling
in her shaking hands.

Drunkenness wants to burn,
races to outlast the night—
shame sneaks up back steps
before the morning light.

While drunkenness loves to fight,
heedless of who or when,
shame fights not to love
and vows *never again.*

Drunkenness loves self-pity,
heard in his howls and moans.
Shame also loves self-pity.
She laps her wounds alone.

Drunkenness saturates fences.
He pisses, never pees,
while shame perches on toilets,
her head between her knees.

Though drunkenness and shame
both start at our corner bar,
both come down our alley.
Neither gets too far.

As much as I love drunkenness
and ruining my own name,
tomorrow we rise early.
Tonight please give us shame.

Bricks

Tennessee Williams called St. Louis bricks
the color of "dried blood and mustard," never
revisited this city once he'd left,
but we can't resist fall evenings here, walking
down damp brick walks by stacks of bricks arranged
into these graceful two- and three-story
Victorian homes. September rain in streetlight
silvers the cypress needles, scatters new dimes
among the nuisance alley mulberry trees.
Ripe wet clay and newly moldering leaves
greet us at every block, and the air is thick
with the sense that all of us, even transplanted
and disappointed, must find something to love
in where we live, if only for an evening.
We cross the highway to the neighborhood
we left last year, decide to take a look
at our old house, spy on the new neighbors.
The Japanese maple waits out back, its leaves
a crowd of burgundy hands waving hello.
We never liked the couple who bought our house
and made the transaction petty, rancorous,
but we had no idea they were so heartless
until we saw the huge forsythia
gone. That old bush almost as old as the house,
a hundred years, grown the size of a school bus,
blazed up each spring in one brief moment no
one happened to be watching, tongues of yellow

fury shooting through the wrought-iron fence.
Days later it wilted, sodden with itself,
a litter of petals curling in the sun,
and looking at the barren earth and stump,
once home to generations of alley cats,
I stand in the vacant lot across the street
and consider heaving one St. Louis brick
through our old home's front window—not even
TV blue but shuttered now light-tight—
not from a sentimental loss of the past
or trespasses on what were once our joys
but for all the wasted beauty of the world.

3. Winter's Bloom

Wild Turkey in January

You stalk this frozen stretch of highway shoulder
between civilizations—Milam Landfill
and Cahokia Mounds. Both rise a hundred feet
to bone-white skies, the biggest man-made mounds
in North America. Cahokia kings
donned cloaks made of your feathers, and today
you pose on bourbon bottles that make us
so crazy we throw rocks at our own homes.

Dreary peacock with spurs and stick-on eyes,
you strut then hide behind your stringy hens.
Ben Franklin thought you nobler than the eagle,
that thief unfit to symbolize our nation.
No others wanted you except stuffed.

We packed your kin so full of corn and hormones
that they can barely stand on three-toed feet,
but you, scrawny and black, look like you staggered
onto the shore from an arctic oil spill,
grizzled feathers glistening in dull sun,
and yet you fly five miles above the speed limit.

O omnivore, polygamist if quick,
snood draped over your beak like a spent condom,
you fly from hate to fear to lust at a rustle
of feathers, leaves, your head a porn-king's cock,
swollen blue from red, wattle turned red
to white, puffing our star-spangled banner.

Seven-faced bird, fire-chicken—Greeks
call you French Chicken, French thought you Indian
who call you Peruvian while Arabs named
you Roman rooster, and Egyptians call
you Greek. The Miami call you native fowl
because you're ours. You're here and everywhere,
wanted or not. Your cackles and tom gobbles
sound like a laugh track, and your fighting purr
blurts like a party horn, one strangled note
to ring in the new year on a cold day.

Ode to Despair

My love-biting friend with no benefits,
never leave. Never stop sucking me dry.

You unleash the loveliest avalanche
of sobs—and in its wake, splendid muffled

desolation. How'd I live without you,
ma chère, snug and delicate as shadow?

Faithful one—after my second marriage
dissolves, we pick up right where we left off.

I once mailed a dear old friend, who shared you
as our lover, a pennant emblazoned

with your name, DESPAIR!, our alma mater.
She crooned on the phone it was the best gift

she'd ever received. A few years later
she died and willed her little flag to me,

who has yet to visit her tidy grave.
Despair pornography: driving past rows

of boarded-up homes, monuments to you.
You make the void seductive, sacred hole.

I love how you sludge through my veins, my brain,
like a slow, poisonous milkshake, nurture

the vague urge to oblivion and yet
never quite release me to death's dull pull.

You ask nothing of me except to choose
your love when there is nothing else to choose.

Bloom of Light: Winter Spell to Revitalize Your Spirit When Days Are Dark and Gloom Settles Upon You

materials: 1-yard diameter circle of yellow cloth
cut from never-used baby blanket
1 vial of blood-red St. John's wort oil
6 candles, 3 yellow and 3 white
2 yellow toadflax or celandine flowers

At dawn, sit in the center of yellow cloth, facing east. Plant candles in circle at edge of cloth, alternating colors. Light and anoint each candle with one drop of oil. Hold one flower in each upright palm, honing your mind on the candles' glow, and chant:

Reviving light, surround me now,
relieve my spirit's darkest hour.
The frozen earth and brittle bough
will never quell your glowing flower.

Gray skies, gray road, cold root, gray bark—
oh bloom of day inside this night,
dispatch the cold, absolve the dark,
let blackness fuel your blazing light.

Envelop me in yellow bloom
and muffle winter's rasp and moan
then banish every crumb of gloom
from every joint and fingerbone.

Let darkness find another day
and blackness witness my rebirth.
Now drop these flowers where they may,
return them to forgiving earth.

Double Helix

His dad had kicked him down the hallway.
His tailbone won't let him forget,
at 50, his twisted DNA.

In tumbling cowboy boot ballet,
smoke curling from a cigarette,
his dad had kicked him down the hallway.

He'd flown, light as papier-mâché,
too slow to dodge the booted threat
and later the twisted DNA,

wishing the mirror on the wall
opened to different wings, would let
him hide down alternate new hallways.

He feared the recoiling spring's delay
and vowed that he would never set
hand, foot, or twisted DNA

against his own. He'd rather crawl
to his grave alone than ever beget.
His dad had kicked him down the hallway
and helped twist off their DNA.

The Ugliest Woman Sitting at the Bar

The ugliest woman sitting at the bar,
her mouth a gash of lipstick, eyes too wide,
hunches into herself like a collapsed star.

Even her gummy smile will never mar
her ugliness, though every night she's tried.
The ugliest woman sitting at the bar,

her bedroom more a tomb than a boudoir,
watches the cloying couples, a life denied,
hunched over rum and coke like a collapsed star.

She laughs but knows what unspoken insults are,
makes all the pretty boys turn ugly inside.
The ugliest woman braced against the bar,

which fills with enough smoke and steel guitar
and drunken strangers for her almost to hide,
smolders on her stool like a collapsed star.

At last, half drunk, she stumbles to her car.
No one checks on or accompanies outside
the ugliest woman sitting at the bar,
her seat empty and black as a collapsed star.

Ode to the Brown-Banded Cockroach

You scuttle on translucent legs at night.
By day you hide behind our picture frames,
in ceiling fans—wait motionless for hours.
You know the art of waiting since you evolved
300 million years before we did.
Of course you eat each other's shit—you need
protozoa to digest our history.

O crazy bug, whose fine-tuned zig meets zag,
your one long brain shoots through your body, head
to rear-end motion detector, calibrated
three knees on all six legs to register
faintest vibrations, warn of boot and broom.
You taste outside your body to avoid
our poisons. You live and live. You find in flames
the safe spot of the microwave and live.

Mama Cockroach, you mate but once in life
then spawn 600 children in a year,
tote perfect tic-tac capsules full of eggs
before you seal them to our kitchen cabinets,
a molting nest of legs, spent shells, and spit.

Once friends invited us to their apartment
to help make cookies for the holidays.
With oven warming, merrily we rolled
and cut our favorite shapes and decorated
in the living room where there was space to work.
We stepped into the kitchen. Hoards of you
had spread from the heat like shrapnel from a bomb
across the ceiling, floor, and walls, thousands
of patient minds suspended above the tile.
"We hadn't used the oven yet," they said.
I watched this constellation in negative
and glimpsed the future, when we destroy ourselves.
O little beans of typhoid, dysentery,
your blood runs clear and irrepressible,
as you wait in our shadow, unblinking eyes,
antennae trembling on the infinite.

Please Be Advised

You are being watched for your protection—
and we protect you everywhere, recorded
for your convenience. Please wait for inspection.

We even track your chewing gum selection
so all your purchases can be rewarded.
You are being taped. For your protection

we monitor each Internet erection.
We know your deepest wants, however sordid.
For your convenience, please spread for inspection.

Wait, hurry. You must not miss your connection.
There is no jumping off this plane once boarded.
You are being locked in for your protection.

Your shadow in shade will not escape detection.
Be grateful for the kindness we've afforded.
For your convenience, please permit inspection.

We have even captured your reflection.
Pay no attention how this form is worded.
Sign on the broken line for your protection,
for your convenience, submitting to inspection.

Stopping for Lunch Near Goshen, Indiana

Their buggy parked between the Taco Bell
dumpster and my ticking Mitsubishi,
an Amish couple feeds on Enchiritos.
She's seventeen and won't make eye contact,
and though her husband will, he never smiles,
brooding on snowflakes swirling in the lot.
His boots and ice-blue eyes make any girl
with hormones wish for *rumspringa*.
A few miles south on Highway 69,
a sign outside the megachurch flashes
"Sinners Welcome!" Inside, the penitent
have KFC and Starbucks. A JumboTron
montages evidence their god hates gays
while jihadists, on a server in the heartland,
post articles on how to disperse a crowd
in smoke and pieces with ingredients
from mom's kitchen and $20 phones.
Technology enables our worst instincts,
religion sanctions them, and so we rose
from cooking fires to huddle round blue screens,
the most seductive and merciless of gods,
which the Amish couple will not own but watches
like I do vixens in mini-skirts the size
of cocktail napkins slink down grocery aisles.
"Land a Goshen!" our elders used to say.
The day darkens with snow. Fat flakes fill up
the parking lot. Their mule stamps out the cold,

but footage of the Middle East, the carnage
wrought by an angry god, the sexy car
and beer commercials, ads for Burger King
won't let them look away. Until they must.
We all must, and so the couple trudges through
the parking lot and takes the highway home.
In back of their buggy a red and orange warning
triangle glares through veils of snowflakes falling
faster now like ghostly little hands.

4. Spring Necromancies

Ode to Big Muddy Asian Carp

An angler's hatred for you is instinctive.
You've spawned and spread up every confluence,
and here, below the Alton lock and dam,
you litter broken concrete shores by thousands,
yanked from your riverbeds and lined like missiles,
some six feet long and some the size of loaves.

You all wear the same face: wide-eyed dismay.
Thistles of bones break through your silver skin
while mounds of guts shine in glorious rot.
No gulls swoop down to pick your eyes or innards.
Though you've been prized through Chinese dynasties
and sold to Israel as gefilte fish,
no one here will touch your flesh but flies
whose maggots boil between your sun-warmed gills.

Over a hundred feet above your stink,
flocks of American white pelicans
caress the currents with their ink-tipped wings.
They pause a moment, studying, then plunge,
a sweeping signature of life and death,
while great blue herons nod to lapping tides.

We brought you here to binge on catfish algae,
but carnage on these banks is your rank triumph,
a florid waste, a drop in the bait bucket
of your relentless population, nudging

out native bluegill, walleye, largemouth bass.
Your silver hoards gleam through our silt waters,
propelled through dams, twisting round each bend
to leap upriver and choke life at the source.

Picnic Pavilion in a State Park

The woods almost forget that he is there.
He watches like a hunter from the hill—
miles of gray branches flexing buds but bare,
his stranger driving through the morning chill.
In seconds they undress beside the sweetgum
and sting each other's nerve-endings with pleasure.
They always leave the pavilion as they come—
separate and wordless, a defensive measure.
This weekend brings the season's family picnics,
but now—the slow parade of whores and hustle
and sneaking off from work for trysts or tricks,
for the human heart's a predatory muscle
that lies in wait on moldering forest floors
where ferns uncoil and morels launch their spores.

Man Accidentally Locks Himself in Basement

After your eyes open up
                   to darkness,
you notice shadows
                   overlapping shadows,
layers of shade
                   along the limestone walls.
Spiders forget
                   you're sitting on the steps,
stop sulking
                   in their corners, rappel from rafters,
continue
                   speculating over their dead.

The walls relax,
                   go back to flecking crumbs,
and cardboard boxes
                   breathe sighs of relief.
A siren tunnels through
                   the earth and stone,
and pungent rot becomes
                   familiar must.
You haven't tried the knob
                   again all day.

You drift and dream
                    of tree roots knocking against
the stone foundation,
                       and then your cell phone rings—
the small light banishes
                     your reverie
back to the Erebus of your
                      own mind.
The other side holds gibberish
                       and static,
and you turn off the phone
                      because nothing
travels through the air
                    down here except
for spider trails
               and quiet expirations.

Surprise

Her face so face-lifted her eyebrows rise,
she sits throughout her son's seventh grade choir
performance with a constant look of surprise.
Back home she sloughs her black evening attire
and piece by piece her diamond jewelry
(her face expressionless but still surprised).
Her husband's fuckery and foolery
bore her almost to tears. Botox has disguised
the worry lines. She feels the whole house shudder
when the AC kicks on, hears him moan and mutter
beside her in his sleep. She rises and pees
repeatedly while he snores all night through,
and morning stains the sky above the trees
a positive home pregnancy test blue.

Gossip

It wets our willies
and tickles the tongue.
It's wires on which
our stories are hung.

Old fashioned gossip:
mosquito-nosed birds
who spread over fences
infectious words.

It's jealous half-lies
and full-blown wishes
through headlines and phone lines
and satellite dishes.

Gossip is glue,
sublime and grotesque—
who's doing who
on the secretary's desk.

It's nibbled with tea
or gobbled with beer.
It's bourbon-breathed
and vodka clear.

Gossip's the chain
that yanks us back when
we stray—or if too far
won't let us back in.

Of course, when we're pressed
we always agree
that gossip is best
when it's not about me.

On gossip's high wire
we rise or we totter.
It's the stones of all culture,
our bread and our water.

Overture from *The Lost City*

for Huayna Capac, the last great Inca, died 1527,
mummified and worshipped after his death and
frequently consulted by his descendants

The sun, the moon,
the mountains, rain—
all our gods forsook us except for one,
Supay, the greedy god, the god of death.
Inti, the sun,
Chiqui Illapa,
the thunder god of rain, Apu, the mountain—
a hundred children sacrificed a year
could not content Supay. Mama Kuka
did not ignore us: the wanton goddess ripped
in half by lovers,
her body grew
into the coca
plant, cocaine.

We crossed rope bridges up to Vilcapampa,
a fortress city hidden in the mountains,
and held the Spaniards off 35 years.
I brought with me my Virgins of the Sun.
The Spaniards raped and killed them, every one.

Conquistadors
with black-robed priests—
their armor gleamed
like silver beasts.

I dreamt of lightning flashing from my feet—
an omen for disease, then came the plagues.
The eagle chased by smaller birds of prey

dropped down into the center of the square,
its body featherless and riddled with scabs,
foretelling earthquakes, floods, and civil war.

We lived on red potatoes, squash, and maize.
They found us from the smoke of cooking fires,
left not one yellowed stone upon another.
We knelt to face the sun and prayed for peace.
They burned us all in piles of ash and grease.

Wind burned our eyes
and chafed our cheeks
when it whipped through
the mountain peaks,

but we survived
in cold, thin air
with hidden paths
and wind-tossed prayer.

The moon had three great haloes—one blood red,
one shaded black to green, the final ashen.
The ancient oracle was true:

Strange peoples of a kind not seen before
would rob the Inca of his empire and leave
behind a calendar of empty days.

The mountains crouch unmoved.
The sun dies slow and silent.
But we must love the world,
the gentle and the violent,
the kindling and new bud.
For all is not in vain
and we must love the world
for there is still the rain,
which stirs our ash to mud,
reconstitutes our blood,
and runs through dead empires,
over rock and rotting tree,
past ruin and dying fires,
and spills into the sea.

Necromancy Spell

materials: 1 cup or mug belonging to the departed
spring rain water
first growth of lavender
orris root
several drops of virgin's blood
7 amaranth flowers
something from the departed (hair
from a brush, fingernail
clippings, ashes if cremated)

*This spell must be performed in spring, at midnight, under
a waxing moon. From favorite cup or mug of the departed,
pour three cups of spring rain water into cauldron. Add rest of
ingredients and boil until fragrant. Facing north and kneeling
from pity, invoke the following:*

Sleeping spirit, speak to me
over the spongy wall of death.
Assume a form that I can see
and breathe with bloodless voice my breath.

Remember when this world spread
its arms in leaf and waves and stones,
embraced the living, spurned the dead,
back when you hugged your blood and bones.

Recall how once your world flowed
with blood and sap and melting streams,
before the endless empty road
of death a moment's flesh redeems.

Death nuzzles young in winter dens,
emerges with the April thaw.
Death gazes from the camera lens,
gleams in the teeth of a rusty saw.

Dead starlight shines through shrouded skies.
Death stretches when bones pop and creak,
but you are wanted back, so rise
from death's unfathomed sea and speak.

April Morning

When the taste of a former lover
has finally vanished from your tongue,
like the moon dissolved in the morning sky,

and no leaves stir in the damp stillness—
though you imagine buds strain
against the chill, trees thicken,
and roots flex underground—

when Monday traffic begins its slush
along the highway, and you have measured
your mornings since the breakup
in toothpaste tubes, deodorants worn to nubs,

you'll know that life knows not how it began,
and spring happened not
in a moment we perceived
but moments slowly recollected

in the ancient smell of rot and bloom,
and even your former lover
appears more beautiful than you remembered.

Bellefontaine Cemetery

Death, however,
is a spongy wall,
is a sticky river,
is nothing at all.

—Edna St. Vincent Millay

1. Jennings

We eat pulled pork while death sprawls at our feet
in the heart of this old boomtown of the dead,
314 acres of time-smoothed tombs
and sinking mausoleums circumscribed
by the empty streets of Jennings, North St. Louis.
Death is a grassy mound, an empty day.

And once a year we bring brown fat-stained bags
of meat, both boned and clinging to its bones,
from Roper's Ribs by the boarded grocery store
and Goodwill, halfway between our campuses.
It's time enough to catch up on the kids
we've known since birth and remember why we're friends

and time to mourn the younger generation's
skull-scratching lack of curiosity,
as older generations once mourned ours—
each class unschooled in its insignificance,
the row on row of faces sandblasted
with stupidity. We gnaw on bones and laugh.

In 1849 the city moved
the graves from the park my home now overlooks
to where they thought St. Louis would settle least,
a month before cholera swept up river
from New Orleans and wiped out ten percent
of the city—virgin fields for stones and bones.

But now it's spring. Semesters sputter out.
Cumulus clouds tower in the sky,
reminding us of pictures from the Hubble,
The Pillars of Creation and *Hourglass*—
far nebulae a billion light-years wide.
Below us, most of the bodies lie preserved

until the world's end. In all these years
of lunches, we've never once seen visitors.
Forgotten histories nudge us into
our future, while crosses, anchors, angels, stars
weather down to nubs and groundskeepers mow
the sixty acres remaining to be filled.

2. In

Seeds tremble in the withered flowers,
dry flowers in a mound.
The wind stirs in the ancient trees,
a box of bones in the ground.

There's flooding in the drops of rain
and cleansing in the flood.
There's rust inside the wrought-iron gates
and iron in the blood.

Black veins and red lie in the marble.
Our code lies in the limestone.
Recorded bells ring in the steeple
and silence in the chime's tone.

Petroleum in the garden soil
will seep into these lakes,
and there's an end in Eden Terrace
and good in garden snakes.

There's poison in the peace lily,
succulence in the cactus,
a monolith in bedside manner,
and mercy in malpractice.

There's weariness in my own eyes,
an ache in every urge,
bitterness in the passion fruit,
and sweetness in a dirge.

There's joy in life, nothing in death,
and sadness when we part,
and there is love, yet never enough,
in my old rotting heart.

3. Graveyard Cottonwood

The ancient cottonwood's diaspora
collects along stone paths and tombs in drifts,
wispy fulfillment that billows, clings, then shifts
across the mossy graves like snowflake flora.
The parachuted seeds blow from the east,
cobwebbing graveyard grass that's rarely mown,
ivies both on the ground and carved in stone.
The tree stands here like some druidic priest,
trunk wrinkled as if draped in ancient robes,
thick up-raised limbs towering above
headstones and monoliths, launching in waves
thousands of wasted worlds, ephemeral globes,
random and delicate as youthful love,
a loose-knit shawl to cover chilly graves.

4. Advice to the Youth of America

All teenagers should party on people's graves,
not worry about waking a sleeping soul
but swill death's foamy drink and ride death's waves.

Every kid should share a few close shaves
with county sheriffs, the local cop patrol.
All teenagers should party on people's graves.

Bring instruments but no PA, no raves.
Cheap beer is as important as birth control,
so swill death's foamy drink and ride death's waves.

When we were kids, we learned how the world behaves—
it honored the spirit of our class asshole.
As teenagers we partied on his grave.

The church sign glows *Jesus Completely Saves!*
Don't save your life for death. Live it whole
and swill death's foamy drink and ride death's waves.

All plots end here, and shattered glass paves
the road to boneyards chewed by worm, rat, mole.
All teenagers should party on people's graves
and swill death's foamy drink and ride death's waves.

5. Out

The briar rose grows out of rock.
The thorn grows out of leaf.
The maggots grow out of the corpse,
detachment out of grief.

In the flood of '93 the dead
slipped out of their muddy graves,
and corpses rolled out of the caskets,
floating on chocolaty waves.

Smoke spews out the crematory,
and ash sifts out of the sky.
The cars pull out of the iron gates.
No good comes out of goodbye.

The brown recluse creeps in and out
of outhouse, basement, tomb.
The quarry's out of marble slabs.
The graveyard's out of room.

We suck the soil and spit the rest out
the muddy mouth of the Missouri.
The outcasts too good for this world
always get out in a hurry.

We never run out of punishments
to fit our earthly crime.
There's laughter to wring out of this old world
as we run out of time.

6. Bones

After our lunch we wipe our hands on grass
then stretch our legs across the spongy graves.
We toss our trash and scatter the bones for rats,
a kettle of turkey vultures overhead.

The earth gives in, uneven from the moles
tunneling runes for blind gods to finger.
We joke that we're the only white people
for miles. At least alive. At least for now.

We both believe in nothing after death
but what the living gradually forget,
and we plod past the celebrated bones—
Adolphus Busch the beer king, William Clark,

barely remembered poet Sara Teasdale—
their graves unvisited except by gawkers
like us who come to marvel at the sculpture,
the architecture, a few words carved in stone.

Regretting we only do this once a year,
we curse the time we waste with all the people
we neither love nor trust, picking our way
through a stand of tombstones weathered wafer thin,

like teeth of those same blind and gaping gods,
and all the names and dates, the scraps of prayer,
have washed back into the spongy earth to leave
these vague stone gestures showing we once lived.

RICHARD NEWMAN is the author of the poetry collections *Domestic Fugues* (Steel Toe Books, 2009) and *Borrowed Towns* (Word Press, 2005), as well as several poetry chapbooks. His poems have appeared in *Best American Poetry, Boulevard, Crab Orchard Review, Measure, New Letters, Poems & Plays, Poetry Daily, The Sun, Unsplendid, Verse Daily,* and many other periodicals and anthologies. His poem "Bellefontaine Cemetery" won first place in The 2010 Ledge Poetry Awards. He lives in St. Louis, where he reviews books for the *St. Louis Post-Dispatch* and edits *River Styx.*

Photo by Chas Adams

ALSO FROM ABLE MUSE PRESS

Melissa Balmain, *Walking in on People - Poems*

William Baer, *Times Square and Other Stories*

Ben Berman, *Strange Borderlands - Poems*

Michael Cantor, *Life in the Second Circle - Poems*

Catherine Chandler, *Lines of Flight - Poems*

William Conelly, *Uncontested Grounds - Poems*

Maryann Corbett, *Credo for the Checkout Line in Winter - Poems*

John Drury, *Sea Level Rising - Poems*

D.R. Goodman, *Greed: A Confession - Poems*

Margaret Ann Griffiths, *Grasshopper - The Poetry of M A Griffiths*

Ellen Kaufman, *House Music - Poems*

Carol Light, *Heaven from Steam - Poems*

April Lindner, *This Bed Our Bodies Shaped - Poems*

Martin McGovern, *Bad Fame - Poems*

Jeredith Merrin, *Cup - Poems*

Frank Osen, *Virtue, Big as Sin - Poems*

Alexander Pepple (Editor), *Able Muse Anthology*

Alexander Pepple (Editor), *Able Muse - a review of poetry, prose & art* (semiannual issues, Winter 2010 onward)

James Pollock, *Sailing to Babylon - Poems*

Aaron Poochigian, *The Cosmic Purr - Poems*

Stephen Scaer, *Pumpkin Chucking - Poems*

Hollis Seamon, *Corporeality - Stories*

Matthew Buckley Smith, *Dirge for an Imaginary World - Poems*

Barbara Ellen Sorensen, *Compositions of the Dead Playing Flutes - Poems*

Wendy Videlock, *The Dark Gnu and Other Poems*

Wendy Videlock, *Nevertheless - Poems*

Wendy Videlock, *Only an Echo - Poems*

Richard Wakefield, *A Vertical Mile - Poems*

Chelsea Woodard, *Vellum - Poems*

www.ablemusepress.com

CPSIA information can be obtained
at www.ICGtesting.com
Printed in the USA
FSOW01n0904101014
3226FS